Need It or Want It?

Colleen Hord

rourkeeducationalmedia.com

www.rourkeeducationalmedia.com

PHOTO CREDITS: Cover: © Waxart, Yen Hung Lin; Title Page: © iofoto; Page 3: © Ashok Rodrigues; Page 5: © monkeybusinessimages; Page 7: © Suprijono Suharjoto; Page 9: © Jason Lugo; Page 11: © Cliff Parnell; Page 13: © mangostock; Page 15: © Christina Richards; Page 17: © ; Page 19: © Igor Strukov; Page 21: © Skip ODonnell, Robyn Mackenzie, Carlosalvarez, scubabartek;

Edited by Meg Greve

Cover design by Tara Ramo
Interior design by Renee Brady

Library of Congress Cataloging-in-Publication Data

Hord, Colleen
 Need It or Want It? / Colleen Hord.
     p. cm. -- (Little World Social Studies)
 Includes bibliographical references and index.
 ISBN 978-1-61741-793-1 (hard cover) (alk. paper)
 ISBN 978-1-61741-995-9 (soft cover)
 Library of Congress Control Number: 2011925063

Rourke Educational Media
Printed in the United States of America,
North Mankato, Minnesota

rourkeeducationalmedia.com

customerservice@rourkeeducationalmedia.com   •   PO Box 643328 Vero Beach, Florida 32964

Do you know the difference between a **need** and a **want**?

A need is something you must have to live a safe and healthy life. Food, clothing, and **shelter** are examples of needs.

A want is something you would like to have, but do not need to survive. A new video game is an example of a want.

Sometimes you see a new toy on TV and think you really need it. You can be safe and healthy without new toys.

Fact

More than 2 billion dollars a year are spent on ads directed toward kids. These ads make you think you need the products.

When you have enough food, shelter, and clothes, your family can shop to buy extra things you want, like new toys.

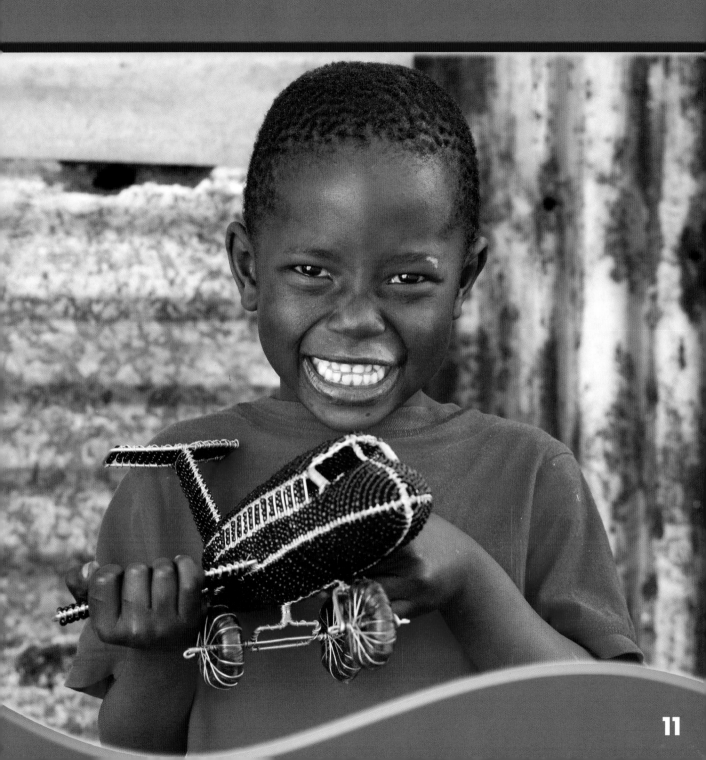

There are some people in your **community** who need food or clothes. You can help by **donating** clothes or food to **donation centers**.

Fact

Food pantries provide food for people who cannot afford it. Food banks are warehouses that give food to the pantries.

DONATION BOX

Donation centers help people get food and clothes when they don't have enough money to buy the things they need.

You can help by donating clothes and shoes you have outgrown or no longer wear.

You are a responsible community member when you help others get things they need.

You can also help others get the things they want. You can donate toys or games.

You can donate some toys you no longer play with to a homeless shelter.

It feels good to help others get the things they need and want!

What do you need? What do you want?

Picture Glossary

 **community** (kuh-MYOO-nuh-tee): A place where a group of people live, work, and care for each other.

 **donating** (DOH-nate-ing): Giving something to someone as a gift.

 **donation centers** (doh-NEY-shuhn SEN-turs): Places where people can give clothing and food to people in need.

need (NEED): Something that you have to have to be safe and healthy.

shelter (SHEL-tur): A home or place to live.

want (WANT): Something that you want to have, but you don't need to be healthy and safe.

Index

Websites

www.kidscanmakeadifference.com
www.jfklibrary.com
www.kids.gov

About the Author

Colleen Hord lives on a small farm with her husband, llamas, chickens, and cats. She enjoys kayaking, camping, walking on the beach, and reading to her grandchildren.

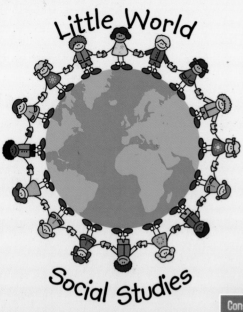

Little World Social Studies

Are you a producer or consumer? Do you have a role in your community? This series is filled with real world examples that will teach you about everything from how you might be a producer or a consumer to what it means to be a good citizen in your community.

Books In This Series Include:

Consumers and Producers

Goods or Services?

Moving People, Moving Stuff

Need It or Want It?

What's My Role?

My Safe Community

Rourke
Educational Media

rourkeeducationalmedia.com

¿Qué necesito?

MI MUNDO

Bobbie Kalman